I Make Jokes When I'm Devastated

Also by Luisa Muradyan

American Radiance

I Make Jokes When I'm Devastated

Luisa Muradyan

Bridwell Press
Southern Methodist University
Dallas, Texas

Bridwell Press is the professional publishing arm of Bridwell Library
(SMU Libraries and Perkins School of Theology).
Southern Methodist University

SMU Libraries SMU Perkins School of Theology

Series Editor: Katie Condon
Design by Alicia Beebe

Printed in the United States of America

ISBN: 978-1-957946-27-6 (hardcover)
ISBN: 978-1-957946-28-3 (paperback)
ISBN: 978-1-957946-29-0 (epub)

Cover image: *Tanks in the heads*, 2019 by Pavlo Borshchenko

For my family

TABLE OF CONTENTS

Into Oblivion

Someone has accidentally set the forest on fire
and having clocked in for the day I turn
this catastrophe into a little poem.
Some days writing feels like this
an animal presents itself to you
and asks to be remembered
maybe the rabbit chewing dandelions in your yard
or the bat gliding over your head in the auditorium.
As much as you may want to move on, the animals
will follow. Today is a quiet day and I am stuck
checking inventory. The things I don't want to remember
I shove in drawers that no one will open,
memories where I was harmed,
no, memories where I was loved.
At the market in Odesa
my grandfather waits for me.
It is my turn to haggle over
the price of strawberries,
once again I am too American
for this moment, he wants me to
do what I have been taught to do
he wants me to survive. He is of course
dead, leading me through this life
by hiding images throughout the world,
used paper towels that I have learned to

fold and store beneath the sink, half-rotten tea
bags that I will return to the soil, and pickle
jars that now hold soup and rainwater.
Back at the market, I follow my grandfather
through the meat section and stop
at the butchered animals
be specific he tells me
and I return to my desk
to write about the concrete apartment
building where my grandfather
watered white roses on our balcony
in Odesa, where bombs now fly
into buildings, into *this building*
into the cracked sink
and pictures of dead

relatives and the rug nailed
to the wall that my father
smuggled on a train
from Czechoslovakia
and the books, and the old
domino set with the carving
of the naked woman on the
cover, tits out and bush on fire
and oh the crystal shot glasses
those only remnants from my grandfather's
wedding, the day he married a woman
who made the best syrniki in the world.
Here,

sit down and eat.

Don't Write Mom Poems

The best writing advice I've ever been given
is to avoid poems about motherhood.
Too sappy. Too sentimental. I agree.
Which is why I only write poems about
myself bare-chested on a hunt,
dragging my latest kill
back to my cabin
and feasting
on what I can
only describe
as truth. No room in this cabin
for a nursery or
a metaphorical child
who sleeps when I
sleep and on waking
looks at me not as creator
but as created, singing some ancient
song in the moonlight.

Woman Posting in Parenting Forum

Friends, I have come to the end of my rope.
My child has decided that he is the moon
and I cannot convince him otherwise. His entire
face a moon, not a man in the moon, but a toddler
that is the moon, and yes he does give off light
in the darkness and yes some days he pulls the ocean
current toward his body and yes I've noticed
that when I take him to poetry readings
or art museums everyone cannot help but stop what
they are doing and begin to draw pictures of him
with images or language and yes there was of course
that one incident where someone shoved an American
flag into his back and yes, it was one small step for the boys
who marked him but a giant leap for me
across the playground and yes there was
that Halloween when he decided to dress like a bat
and a broken superhero showed up on our doorstep
and I had only peanuts to give him
when what he really needed was
purpose, I guess what I'm saying is I don't know
how to parent the moon and now I'm making this about me
because the scientists are telling us that the moon
is drifting away from the Earth and I gotta admit
most days my gravitational pull
is a dilapidated hug at best

and friends did you know
that scientists surmise that the moon was made
when a rock smashed into the Earth
and the more I look at my
son's birth photos the more I see my body
ripped open by my sun, no wait by my
moon who invites me into the space
of his playroom and smiles
with the fullness of his face
And I guess what I'm trying to say
is yes, I have been eclipsed by love.

At the Kansas Flint Hills Museum

my son rips a prairie violet out of the wall. *If he does that again, we will have to ask you to leave.* He wants to save it for later, to hold on to something beautiful. He grabs my hand and marches me over to a sprawling map of the United States. *Where was I born mamma?* I point to Houston, there. *Where there are crocodiles?* Yes, darling. *Where are you from mamma?* I have nowhere to point to. My favorite crocodile is a melancholic cartoon named Gena who plays the accordion. Ukraine is back in the imaginations of my well-meaning acquaintances who fold their faces into the shape of concern and ask how my family is. Somewhere a television is showing stock images of war and all of them are on fire. *How many people will die?* The television doesn't say, and yet I hear the field of wildflowers. Each one has been ripped out of the ground. Somewhere my grandmother sings.

I Make Jokes When I'm Devastated

If you walk the stations of the cross, most tour guides
will politely point out the spot where they think Jesus
may have fallen or the spot where
he may have met his mother.
This holy place may have been a few meters west
or possibly in that gift shop over there.
We live in a world of "close enough":
The missiles that fell on the village
did not directly hit my grandmother's
childhood home, but they were close enough.
The Russian invaders claimed they did not mean
to bomb Babyn Yar, but their shells were close enough.
My great-grandmother wasn't that Jewish,
but she was close enough. When you ask me for
another response to tragedy, I tend to begin with a joke. Which isn't
exactly the shape of sorrow, but I assure you,
it is close enough.

My Mother as Tom Cruise

Or as every other late '80s action hero
my mother successfully jumping off a skyscraper
onto another skyscraper, my mother hunting the
Predator with a cigar lodged in her mouth
my mother saying sonofabitch in the coolest
way imaginable my mother ripping a mask off
to reveal she is not in fact the president of the United
States but that she is in fact my mother
my mother somehow knowing how to pilot
a helicopter my mother pulling her abusive
father out of a bathtub my mother slamming
her fist down on the table during an arm
wrestling tournament my mother registering
her hands as lethal weapons my mother pleading
with her mother to leave before things got dangerous
my mother watching things get dangerous
my mother holding the green wire and the blue
wire and figuring out which wire to cut
my mother covered in her mother's blood
my mother my mother my god my mother
walking away from a burning
car my mother an action hero
that self-destructs and yet she's still
my mother sitting in front of a villain
calmly explaining to him that death

is almost here without sharks without
bombs. My mother pale as the moonlight,
my mother watching him
die slowly, in explosive peace
and immeasurable quiet.

Everything Is Sexy

When the toll booth sign says
Please don't stop
I sigh and say, here we go.
Once again, everything is sexy
and the world wants to swallow
me whole. Pushing D69
on the vending machine? Sexy.
Taking the top off
of the recycling bin?
So sexy. Cracking open an ice-cold
sparkling water with a French-sounding
flavor like pamplemousse? Le Sexy.
And yes maybe it's my hormones trying
to trick me into another iteration of God
be fruitful and multiply
or maybe it's just you tending to the garden
that I promised I would water and never
do and yet here you are in your gray
gym shorts and this is the summer
of cucumbers as big as my want
and I'm holding an empty salad bowl
waiting for you to come inside.

When I Say I Am Not the Speaker of My Poems

I mean I am absolutely the speaker of my poems.
I mean that after a long day of being alive
I will take my bra off in the least sexy way possible

and tell you every embarrassing story that has ever happened to me
like how in sixth grade I took the *Seventeen* magazine quiz
and found out how to be a lady in the streets, and a freak in the sheets

or how the boy I liked rejected me on
Submarine Pizza Day and yes
my heart did sink and yes I care

more than I should and yes sometimes
I am the wheel and sometimes the hamster
running desperately out of my cage.

When I say I am not the speaker of my poems
I mean I am a Halloween decoration
that has been left out too long and is now made to be merry.

When I say I am not the speaker of my poems
I mean that I am three small forest creatures walking into
your party in a trench coat.

I mean I am a Jell-O mold
floating in a sea of jellyfish.
I mean that I am not

the three-tier lily-white wedding cake
that you rent for photos but the sheet
cake behind the bar that is ready to do

what is asked of it. When I say I am not
the speaker of my poems I mean that I am
the mall Santa smoking cigarettes on my lunch break,

I mean I am the one who will tell you
what you want to hear. What do you
want to hear?

I'll cut every emotion
out of construction paper
and hang a garland in your craft room.

When I say I am not the speaker of my poems I mean that I am
a celebrity looking at myself in a wax museum unsure
of which one of us deserves to be loved.

Light Crimes, A Love Story

It was our second week in the United States and my mother needed to learn how to drive so she could get a job mopping floors. My father borrowed a white van from the community center where he mopped floors and boiled spaghetti on Italian night. And maybe you don't see it at first but this story is romantic. The middle of the night, two young immigrants in love in an alleyway, matching leather jackets, and my mother's red lips shining in the moonlight? No, not shining but radiating like a neon sign that said open. Did she scratch the car on purpose or was she unsure of how to parallel park? The answer didn't matter because the next day my sleepless father followed the driving test instructor. Noted the 25 feet marked by orange cones and knew he could not teach my mother how to place a vehicle between them. You see she was not born to fit into arbitrary spaces, she needed room for her hair and her eyes and her voice that my father often says fills a room like an ocean fills a fish tank, immediately until everyone is drowning in beauty. Instead, he committed some light crimes and moved the cones minutes before her turn to take the driving test. And listen, I know you want me to tell you whether or not she passed or whether or not my father was arrested, but all I can say is that she wore her fur coat and aviator sunglasses that day, and my father watched her from that borrowed van thinking she looked Technicolor, an American movie star playing the role of a woman with no way to return home.

Self-Portrait as Midwestern Grocery Store

As beautiful as an aisle of Jell-O
I am radiant orange, lemon-lime, blue raspberry, and green
grape. I am the entire Garden of Eden in box form,
a powder of pomegranates and apples and I am always
ready for the deli meat section.
The Butterball is the only way
I ever want to think of a turkey
and not the wisdom on the face of the old
hen who would perch herself on a weather vane
in my backyard to remind me
to watch my children
who often wander too close to the forest.
And maybe I'm not cut out
for the real world or the fresh produce
section, which makes sense because I was born
right after Chornobyl exploded. And now
I'm in the candle aisle again
and I just can't leave. A place of smells
where we replace reality with what we
think it should be, cucumber melon,
lilac spring, vanilla sugar cookie, the smell
of the funeral home where you planned
your grandfather's wake
cedar and sweet caramel.

The warm bologna sandwich
he unwrapped from his pocket
the day you found out
he was leaving his body behind.

Imagine

You are floating in space
and not in that Sandra Bullock
and George Clooney looking
galactically sexy way
but in that my grandmother
disappeared when I was a child
and I pretended she was
abducted by aliens way

Imagine that science experiment
you did in seventh grade
when the teacher kept adding
pennies into a glass of water
and no matter how much grief
you poured into your body
the surface wouldn't break.

Imagine your grandmother waits for you
in the field of the dead.
You are wearing your purple
dress, she is wearing her purple dress,
the field is wearing its lavender dress.

Imagine being sad only some of the time.
In the spaceship where they took her,
they labeled her *human*
and this fantasy brings you comfort.

Yom Kippur

I know nothing of forgiveness,
it is a yearly tradition
for me to practice and fail
like the sonnet that I still
do not understand how to write.
I could tell you about the time
my mother forgave her father
for a lifetime of destruction.
She meant it enough to spend two hours
trying to pull his half-dead body
out of the bathtub, tearing her shirt
and weeping. In his room a tower
of Russian smut magazines stacked
so high, they almost looked like a steeple.

My Favorite YouTube Channel

think *Beetlejuice* without Michael Keaton
but with one hundred Geena Davises
dressed in floral nightgowns

think absolute freedom

standing in a house
of haunted women

listening to the music
of furniture moving without explanation

in this video, you can see the outline
of a face in the fireplace

everything has burned down again

and I still can't say out loud
the most erotic parts
of the alphabet

a ghost once spelled a dirty word in a Ouija game
and I am convinced it was my childhood
self communicating with my adult self

wasn't I a hilarious six-year-old
telling the jokes of my ancestors

a long line of chickens
terrified
and yet
crossing the road.

At the Rat Casino for Children

I am not interested in cautionary tales
though the only things my grandfather ever bought me
were purchased with casino money.
I have kept each of these relics as reminders of beauty.
This electronic watch was a gift from the Flamingo
and this Most Valuable Player lanyard happens to be
my favorite color and this pocket slot machine was even programmed
to say Happy Birthday, and yes everything is broken everywhere
except here where I find myself comfortable alongside
the permanent melancholy of an animal band. They play our song again,
I hum my tune again, I tell the teenage girl inside of the mouse costume
that I too have had to separate my mind from my body
and we share a moment of knowing before she begins to throw
tickets in the air to appease the crowd of toddlers. Mine is among them
though I can tell he is still unsure about what it means to take.
Hours later we stand quietly at the prize counter and he points
to a tiny eraser that is worth a fortune
that one, your favorite color, Mommy.
I tell him to choose something else, something for himself
and he shakes his head, shakes it hard,
already understanding something about inheritance.

The Joke

My father is a funny man.
What killed him the most
was not being able to make
my mother laugh
in this new language
and no, I'm not talking
about a mayonnaise knock-
knock joke or a chicken crossing
a road, no I'm talking about a real joke
a joke that you don't tell in polite company.
The Midwest is full of manners
but we came from a culture of brutal
intimacy. It took him months of study
months of listening to the men at the factory
tell their jokes during lunchtime
all Pepsi and sandwiches
until he came home one day
shaking and ready.
He sat her down on the good
chair and we huddled around the table
as if we were at a comedy club
You see there was a woman
and a taxi cab and a driver
who tells her
that a man with large feet

has a large penis
and a woman with a small mouth
has a small vagina
And my mother scrunched up her lips tightly
and said
Are you serious?

Another Fire Drill

As we crowd onto the football field
none of us are frightened.
The fire is only in our minds
the possibility of destruction
the forgotten Bunsen burner
the cucumber melon candle
that smells as good as a field
of factories, each one melting
into our minds. We have become
experts at preparing for the end
when the field catches fire
we will go to the street
and when the street catches fire
we will crawl into my car
a blue Toyota Celica that smells
like raspberry body spray
and is full of old homework
assignments, math worksheets
and spelling tests, journal entries
and bad poems. The car is of course
lost to history. What I'm really trying
to say is, it is my job to save us though
I have nothing to carry you but language
and even that has turned into ash.

Ant Farm

It's midnight again and I'm watching the ants
in my son's farm go about their day.
Sometimes I like to give them names
though I often worry I can't keep track of who
is who, or is it whom? Susan and Ted, maybe Barbara
or Dan. I often joke to my husband that if he isn't sure
about the name of one of my relatives he should guess
Natasha or Oleg, Boris or Bogdan, all of them interchangeable
I'm speaking of course of the ants though lately there has been
so much death I don't know myself anymore. I think it was
Barbara who lost her lover somewhere in a tunnel and carried his body
through the field in mourning. Maybe it was Ted, or maybe it was Dan
who my son often notes has the most energy, perhaps the most to prove.
I'm tired of proving to you why Natasha deserves to live, why Oleg once
saved a baby bird who fell out of its nest, though its mother abandoned it
eventually. The birds eye view of the field is trees and dirt, no one knows
how many bodies are silenced underneath. Back in my son's room I sit
like a god and watch them work, wondering if they can see me or
if they believe I am there. If I ever need to destroy them, I will
justify it somehow. Cruelty has its purposes.
Maybe they escaped and wanted to make their home
in mine. Maybe I can dig up old dirt, write in a moral lesson.
But I have nothing to teach them, they know too much of
tragedy and what it is to wait for the end

The Stalin Prize

For Fatima Butaeva

I got the idea
for florescent lamps
from a fire
fly who landed gently
and died in the crease
of my palm.
If you ignite the bulb
you will see a room
full of bodies
stacked like candles
unlit and blinding.
What is science
to a room of fruit
flies? I am born
and will die in the flesh
of a peach. It is all
religion. I believe in light
the way I believe in the lightbulb
the almighty frozen
in glass.

In the Field of the Dead

I have brought the wrong kind of sandwiches
and yes, I know this poem is supposed to bring us there
by river or through a series of ivory clouds,
my grandfather on a bench surrounded by lilies.
But I have brought a turkey sandwich
mustard, tomato slices, lettuce,
when I should have brought bologna,
thick-cut Wonder bread,
wrapped in a saved paper towel.
One that has been cared for,
used to dry hands, tea spills,
something that holds memory.
The sandwich isn't even important,
it is the paper towel that will live forever
my grandfather surrounded by new rolls
that he would never
dream to open.

You Take Your Kids to a Marble Store

And they pick out the ones that will roll
out of your hands, which of course
are full of holes and of course
your son chose one that looks like
the Black Sea and of course
they are still bombing Odesa
and of course you tried to save it
but it ran down your throat
and out of your chest and of course you regret
having a spinning fan installed where you once
had a heart and of course the targeted ads
understand you better than your therapist
tired but funny mom, lost her marbles.
And of course your daughter cried when they
began the marble-making demonstration
frightened of the flamethrower and fistful of
sand on the beach before it was
burned into glass.

On Prayer

I can't prove it, but my father invented the
That's What She Said joke.

His first documented use was during
our naturalization ceremony, mixing up
the *she* and *said* in his broken English
but still making the judge laugh
when he asked my father
if he was *ready for something so big*
as citizenship.

Another instance was when a teacher
told my father that I was too different
and *not quite fitting in.*

Or when a wealthy family
complained that the pizza
he had delivered in the rain
just wasn't hot enough

A trick my therapist taught me
is that when you receive bad news
pretend the sender is a popular
television character.

Michael Scott adjusts his tie
and takes a sip out of his "World's
Best Boss" mug. We stare at each other
a long time. This is the episode where
he doesn't want to be the first to talk,
Michael Scott hates to disappoint people.

Finally, he tells me that my father
has cancer. He tells me, *this is the worst,*
he offers me a hug and I hold back tears
before staring directly into the camera.

In this office, I don't know what else to say
turning toward Michael Scott,
in his white coat, I mumble
grief is just really hard

and he whispers back softly
as if he is reciting a prayer
That's what she said.

Butterflies Remember a Mountain that No Longer Exists

In an attempt to become
a new person, caterpillars
melt their entire bodies
into Jell-O. What is left
of their brain knows only
what it needs to survive
and yet the butterfly brain is haunted.
Echoes tell it to fly
to a home that doesn't exist,
an eroded mountain, burned
down house, bombed
out city. My father tells me
that he will die before
he gets to see Odesa again
And I have nothing to offer
except a memory of him too drunk
to walk but not too drunk to dance
down Derybasivska in the middle
of the night, singing about love
and knocking on every bakery door
until someone opened a window
and offered him fresh verhuny
a pastry often referred to
as *angel wings.*

Instead of Ascending

After Gerald Stern

I was going to write a poem
where I make love to the fields.
I would note that the dandelions
just need someone to blow them
and that grass was best when wet and
bowed over in pleasure
but instead of ascending
into the world of the pastoral
I will behave like a Jew
and mourn the dead bird
in my driveway. A fledgling
who had fallen out of its nest
pushed out by invaders, by those
who would erase its song and
tiny dancing wings. I lay down
next to her and saw the sky how
she saw it. Empty of anything
worth writing about except
of course, the body
of her mother.

Americans Add Jell-O

When you first told me of your mother's
strawberry salad I imaged a subtle
sweetness gently tossed among spinach
leaves and almond slivers. I imagined you
slipping out of your window undetected at
night to chase fireflies in the heat
of summer. I imagined your boyhood
full of adventure, empty boxcars, animals
that needed saving and the occasional lesson
in good-hearted goodness.
When she handed me the bowl
you explained, "Americans add Jell-O,"
radiant cubes dressed in whipped cream
mandarin oranges sliced into quarters.
It was not the first surprise or the last,
though I think about
that salad often, how it tremored
even after it had been placed
on your plate, a memory
you could not control. Even now
I know your childhood was fiction,
more fire than fly, more animal than saving,
more reality than fantasy. And I'm
writing all of this to say that I love you
in a way that is unshakeable.

Standing in the Corner of the Gym at the Valentine's Day Jr. High Dance While all the Kids Scream the Lyrics of "Sweet Caroline"

The boy I like is screaming, the girls who don't like me are screaming, even my teachers who do not know who I am are screaming the chorus. And even though I have been in this country long enough to understand the gist of who Caroline is, I really don't know her or her song, so I gather myself and fill my chest with as much air as possible and I too begin to scream: Bahhh Bahhh Bahhh like a goat who too has been shattered by love. And no this isn't a poem about adolescent crushes or assimilation, this is about how my mother had Alla Pugacheva playing in the car on the drive home and how I could barely piece together a definition of shame though I had already memorized its rhythm.

I Just Need You to Understand that Chickens Are Basically Dinosaurs

When you place the oval head
of your pterodactyl nugget into your ketchup
you walk a thin line of awareness that
I as your parent
do not fully understand.
What meaning can we make of the dead?
The answer is buried deep,
recognizable only after we have made
the thing into what we think
a thing should be.
We don't want to eat a chicken
that looks like a chicken
but a part of our brain knows
that the chicken was once
a dinosaur, was once
a ruler of the world.
It's why we put shoes on the dead
or lip liner where we think the mouth
should go. It's why language is another
kind of container, a shell full
of something we can consume
but never really know.

It's why I should say something beautiful
to you here, but instead I sit
and watch my son anoint his nuggets
with sauce and in this moment
they are holy.

Woman with Cheesecake Factory Menu

I am comforted by the clashing décor,
Greek columns, stained glass, the faint
outline of Anubis by the bar. Was the designer
confused or did they simply want too much?
I want too much both
the fried macaroni and cheese
and the glam burger injected with more
macaroni and cheese, I want you to know
that the bacon bacon cheeseburger
contains no typos. That one bacon wasn't enough and that
here even the chicken parmesan can be ordered pizza-style
and really I'm just talking about that one January
when the city was covered in freshly whipped garlic
mashed potatoes, and yes it was snow
and yes, I want you to still be alive, carrying
a plain cheesecake even though I asked for strawberry
and you said we didn't need anything more than the moon
the only thing we could not find in the book of prayers,
Dead Sea Scrolls sandwiched between faith and bottomless
french fries.

Woman with Hysteria Prescription

Perhaps I should have been embarrassed
when they performed the Pap smear and
the doctor said *Hold on I think I see something!*
and launched his head down the rabbit hole
of my body, but I knew he wouldn't find
a secret garden of lilacs or peony bushes
but a post-apocalyptic landscape
that only a few survivors had escaped from.
What I should have said was *sorry,*
I can't turn the death machine off which seems better
than calling something a babymaker because
my babymaker can't make babies anymore,
but perhaps it can be rewired to make porcelain angels
each one identical but also a collector's item. *Hysterical*
he called me, *No, hilarious,* I told him, as I took what was mine
and descended into the sea.

Maybe I am Tony Soprano

Pleading with Big Pussy
to not betray me though
I have been betrayed before
by so many men with so many
problems and maybe I am just
a little bit insecure.
My robe falling off me as I wade
into the swimming pool with water
birds and maybe I am a little bit in love
with Christopher and Paulie
and maybe I too wear my tracksuits
on days I need to feel the texture
of velour and maybe I just need
to tell my therapist about
the long line of dangerous men
that came before me
like the spaghetti that needs
to be thrown against a wall
to know when it is done,
my grandmother's hair sticking
to brown tile, wet and golden.
I am back in the pool
and there is nothing you can say
to make these birds fly again.

My Mother Insists that I Stop Telling People She Was a Smuggler

You see she would only pay a guy to take some stuff
to a place. It could have been nothing but mostly
it was diamonds and furs, whatever she could get her
hands on. One time it was endless yards of tent material
and what could you even do with that? Pay some other guy
with a sewing machine to make them into pants and jackets.
Look up the spelling for Adidas, make it look
the way it looked that other time your maybe cousin
brought one from Poland. There was of course the one time
she did the carrying herself and that was when
she got caught. Because she wasn't a smuggler,
just a teenage girl with two kilos of black caviar.
You might ask yourself what a smuggler does
when they are caught. And my mother
cannot answer you, she can only
say that she refused to admit what she wasn't.
Instead, she sat on her suitcase
and shoveled caviar into her mouth one handful at a time,
the customs agents staring at her, like fish swimming in fire.

I'm Living Laughing and Loving

it's what I say to the chorus of internet moms.
We've gathered to share our joy,
that Susan found a good deal on felt carrots
to place into her repurposed bowl or that
Annie finally found the right cardigan to wear
to the ice cream social or that Sandy finished
her canvas painting of foliage and forests titled
Fall, and Faith got early access to the friends
and family sale at Old Navy, soon all of us covered
in fleece and enjoying the soft breeze of a revolving door and
just last week Judith posted a photo of the man who
she decapitated with the knife she got on sale at Aldi.
The work of course was difficult and long but
detaching your head from your body is something
most of the women in our group had done before,
violence shiplapped into the walls of the house
that stands on chicken legs
the door that swings open
and apologizes in the moonlight.

Replacing the Zodiac Signs with Atomic Symbols

I always ask
my potential lovers
what their atomic symbol is.

Everyone wants to find a Hydrogen
if they are an Oxygen, but I was not born
for water.

The truth is
I want to be sexy
like Oganesson,
radioactive and unstable
but the electric moon
tells me I am a Boron,
easily found and compounded
often sad, and late to parties.

So rarely do I exist
all on my own,
taking my sweater off
and on in the middle of a Walmart
asking other shoppers to find
the restart button on the back
of my spine.

I was made out of pain
or to put it erotically,
my mother erupted
in nucleosynthesis.

I am often told to wait
for Boron season
when I will be at my most
florescent, bright, bonded

and alive
screaming about the end
or maybe the beginning
ready to hand you a pocket
periodic table so that you too
could know the composition
of oxidized truth.

He Didn't Know How He Started This Habit but He Did

After Linda Pastan

BB gun in hand he would make a sport out of
shooting the squirrels in his yard.
He told his wife this was a form
of stress relief, a way to blow off steam.
At first, it made his neighbors uncomfortable
but they decided it was best to keep quiet
and to their own business.
It wasn't until one night in the dead
of winter when his children saw
the murders taking place
that he finally did what he thought
was the right thing and stopped killing
in the daylight. Of course history
compelled him forward,
burying the bodies in the dark,
where the moon was his only witness.

Self-Portrait as My Mother

We are playing that game again –
She puts her hands on her shoulders
I put my hands on my shoulders
She touches her toes
I touch my toes
She shakes it all around
I shake it all around

*

She is calling her friend in Ukraine
I am calling my friend in Ukraine
She is feeding my child
I am feeding my child
She is using beauty as a sledgehammer
I am telling my crying child that the light-up
shoes he picked out are ugly.
But maybe we should start from the beginning –
I am holding my baby girl
She is holding me on a train
She is pointing to her stretch marks
I am drawing happy faces on my scars

*

Her mother is yelling at her
My mother is yelling at me
She is smiling for a photograph
Someone is paying me for a photograph
She is injecting beauty into her face
I am ripping beauty out of my face
She is pleading with me to stop
I am turning my frown upside down
She looks like her mother

*

I look like my mother
She is pretty as a picture
I am Caravaggio's Judith
She belongs to no one
I belong to everyone
She is standing in the museum
I am explaining this painting to my child –

*

If you study her long enough
you will see the outline of my face.

Thanks for Being Here, Folks

I was going to open it up with a joke
about how women shop too much
but I stopped on the way here to buy
some new material. And really, I am talking
about the fabric of space and how
there aren't enough jokes in the universe
to get me to love myself but I promise you
that I am trying. Did you hear the one where
a woman says something smart? It starts with, "A man
once told me..." And I just need you to admit
that was a little bit funny because there are so many
men who sit in the velvet smoking rooms of the internet
who only see me as the butt of every joke and I do have
a great ass, though I cannot speak to you about the contents
of my chest without first explaining that like a tornado
I too will take your house, like a tornado I too will
moooove your cows across the sky like shooting
stars, like a tornado I too will throw
that gold-framed picture of your father into a field
of wildflowers that, yes are on fire, that yes
burn because of me. You see I have bled for more
than five days and didn't die
and yes I am a thing
that should not be trusted.

Tolstoy Buys Another Horse He Doesn't Need

My favorite review of *War and Peace*
is from an anonymous account
that thought it needed
"More war and less long descriptions
of women."
I am one long description
of women. Blonde hair, brown hair,
hair ripped out of the ground
body like tree body like bush
body like meadow made
of bodies. Body young
and beautiful but also
old body like bog and I'm in the dirt again
asking for nothing but to be transformed.

The Auschwitz Exhibit Asks Me to Rate My Experience

We stand in the grand hall
that last month
was a traveling dinosaur
exhibit, on the wall
where they have now painted
barbed wire, I see traces of what
must have been an outline
of a bone. *What happened to them?*
My grandmother still won't tell me
what she saw in that forest
the next room is a train station
and the next is a ditch we can call
a grave or a horror or
whatever language brought me
to the portrait of a child
the same age as my son.

Midnight Blue

I own exactly nine
crushed velvet Juicy Couture
tracksuits and I have kept each one
as a relic for survival.
Soviet diaspora women
glittering in Swarovski unison,
the rare turquoise teal
that I fished out of the sea
of discount bins, the buttercream
frosted banana that I accidentally
stole from an outlet store in San Marcos,
Texas. Finding the perfect tracksuit is
really a piece of cake. For the woman who is
interested in nature, I recommend a hunter-green
or an ombre sequined sunset. If you only want
to dip your toe in velour then we can start you off
with a modest gray or a cool mint. That was the color I was wearing
when a man on the street called me a Russian whore,
and if I had a tracksuit for every time an academic called me exotic, I
would be the tsarina of tracksuits. I want to be buried
with every stereotype you can think of. Inside my
coffin, there will be a smaller coffin, the papers will call it
a matryoshka laid to rest. And when I die, dress me in the onyx
or midnight blue.

The 800

They had no other races left
to assign me when I joked
that my body was mostly decorative
and yes I was slower than the other runners,
not a natural athlete by any means
though I signed up for track the way
an animal would who was trying
to escape a predator that waited
for her out in the wild. The gold-painted
Ford LTD with broken windows
rolled faster than my legs could take me
as I ran to practice where the chain-link
fence seemed to hold a paradise full
of sweat and dust. What more did I want
back then but to survive? To be as clear
as an empty bottle of Gatorade,
as untouched as the smooth surface of a
rain puddle before galoshes
made the sound of galoshes.
What I'm really trying to say is
if you see me running know that
I am running from a memory
and that with each gasp
I am shoving fistfuls of air
into my lungs like a balloon artist
bending a long appendage
into the shape of joy.

As I Get Closer to Death I Become Full Poem

I often tell my husband
that the strawberries in Odesa
are smaller but sweeter
and these ones we carried in
from Costco are as big
as the American Dream
the size of Texas
and the color of ketchup
which is another American fantasy
that tastes nothing like tomatoes
but has a tinge of blood and sugar.
The strawberries in my memory
aren't of course strawberries at all
they are similes of what was left behind
ripped from the ground like a weed
who could not bear fruit or like a mother
in want of the child that was taken from her.

Quoting the Bible

Tonight I'm thinking about Jesus
which isn't remarkable
for most people on Christmas
but it is for me.
Which means that I'm really
thinking about the light
from Seamus Heaney's phone
when he texted his wife
don't be afraid seconds before
he left his body behind. *Don't be afraid,*
I tell my son as I
buckle his seatbelt, *don't be afraid,*
I place a green dinosaur
mask on his face,
don't be afraid, I spray
his toddler hands with
disinfectant, *don't be afraid,*
I hold him close
and walk away from
other mothers singing
their own version of
don't be afraid
I say it so often
I wonder if my son
thinks the words

are a series
of sounds I hum
when I'm around him
to get through the day
more comfort
than language, more
shape than mouth,
more mother than person,
more memory than body.

Each Month My Grandmother Sends Money to a Stranger Who Puts Flowers on Her Mother's Gravestone in Odesa

There are days I believe that nothing is sacred,
that we will destroy ourselves as a form of hope,
and days when the dead birds in my driveway agree with me.
As a child, I had hoped for something more than this.

But tonight my daughter lets me rock her to sleep.
She too is suspicious of what she will inherit
and wraps her entire hand around my thumb.

I would give anything to take care of you forever.
And I know this too is a lie.
She pays what she can and is sent a photo
each month of a gravestone with fresh lilies.
I can't tell her the stranger
is sending her the same photo. Six lilies,
one green vase, half-broken fence, and the dead
giveaway, the same yellow tail
of a cat, body just out of frame.
When they bombed the cemetery, the picture
of the lilies continued to show up in her
mailbox and I continued to assure her
that this was money well spent.
They, of course, took everything
but these flowers will last forever.

Acknowledgements

Thank you to the editors of the journals below, where many of these poems first appeared, sometimes with slightly altered forms:

Only Poems: "As I Get Closer to Death I Become Full Poem," "Everything Is Sexy," "Instead of Ascending," "Into Oblivion," "Light Crimes, A Love Story," Self-Portrait as Midwestern Grocery Store," "Tolstoy Buys Another Horse He Doesn't Need," "Woman Posting in Parenting Forum," "Woman With Hysteria Prescription"

Threepenny Review: "Don't Write Mom Poems," "My Mother as Tom Cruise," "Quoting the Bible," "I Just Need You to Know that Chickens Are Basically Dinosaurs," "Each Month My Grandmother Sends Money to a Stranger Who Puts Flowers on Her Mother's Gravestone in Odesa"

The Sun: "I Make Jokes When I'm Devastated"

Copper Nickel: "When I Say I Am Not the Speaker of My Poems," "Replacing the Zodiac Signs with Atomic Symbols

PANK: "Imagine," "Yom Kippur"

Missouri Review: "My Favorite YouTube Channel," "The Joke," "Midnight Blue"

Colorado Review: "At the Rat Casino for Children"

Black Warrior Review: "Ant Farm"

Poetry London: "The Stalin Prize"

Guernica: "In the Field of the Dead"

Iowa Review: "On Prayer," "Thanks for Being Here Folks"

Georgia Review: "Butterflies Remember a Mountain that No Longer Exists," "Americans Add Jell-O"

Poetry Ireland: "Standing in the Corner of the Gym at the Valentine's Day Jr. High Dance While All the Kids Scream the Lyrics of Sweet Caroline"

Barrelhouse: "Woman With Cheesecake Factory Menu"

Indianapolis Review: "Maybe I am Tony Soprano"

Oxford Review: "My Mother Insists that I Stop Telling People She Was a Smuggler"

Winning Writers: "I'm Living Laughing and Loving"

Without the love and endless encouragement of my husband, children, parents, and grandparents, this book would not exist. They are my inspiration and my entire world; every page of this book contains their light. Additionally, I'd like to thank my in-laws and siblings for their unending support of my work. I'd also like to thank Kathleen Peirce, without whose mentorship I would not be the poet I am today, and my teachers over the years at Texas State University and the University of Houston. Thanks to my poetry sister Julia Kolchinsky, who is often my first reader, and the members of the Cheburashka Collective, who consistently remind me that I am not to be discarded in a box of oranges. Thanks to my dear friends who worked alongside me over the years and who have consistently read and supported my writing:, Georgia Pearle, Michele Nereim, Erika Jo Brown, Misty Matin, Elizabeth Threadgill, James Knippen, John Andrews, Stephanie Motz, Mary Self, Denise Rodriguez, Ruth Madievsky, Traci Brimhall, Tomas Morin, Ilya Kaminsky, and Kayla Klein.

A special thanks to Pavlo Borshchenko for lending his incredible art to this project.

My deepest gratitude to the amazing Katie Condon and David Caplan for their belief in my poems and this book, as well as Anthony Elia, Elisa Welder McCune, and Alicia Beebe for their brilliance and vision. Additionally, I want to give a heartfelt thanks to the entire staff at Bridwell Press/SMU Project Poëtica at Southern Methodist University for making this dream a reality.

And a final thanks to my ancestors, who built the stage I stand on.